CHRISTIAN NATIONS EAGLE WARRIORS

C.N.E.W.

We do hereby admit to the following beliefs;
By Dr. St. Michael

PRECEPTS NOT KNOWN OR TAUGHT.
VOL. I.

C.N.E.W.

By

Dr. St. Michael

Cadmus Publishing
CadmusPublishing.com

C.N.E.W.

Manufactured in the United States of America. Copyright 2025 by Dr. St. Michael. All rights reserved. No part of this book may be reproduced in any form, audio, digital, or in print, except excerpts by reviewers, without written permission from the copyright holder or Cadmus Publishing LLC.

DISCLAIMER:
    The thoughts, opinions, and expressions herein are those of the author and do not reflect those of Cadmus Publishing LLC. Any similarities to actual events or people are purely coincidental. Names and distinguishing characteristics may have been changed to preserve the identities of any individuals. Published by Cadmus Publishing LLC. P. O. Box 8664. Haledon, NJ 07538

Web: Cadmuspublishing.com
Web: Booksbyprisoners.com
Web: MusicbyPrisoners.com
Facebook.com/Cadmuspublishing
Business email: admin@cadmuspublishing.com
Phone: 360.565.6459

ISBN# 978-1-63751-532-7

Book Catalog Info Categories:
  Religious

Cadmus Publishing
CadmusPublishing.com

C.N.E.W.—Dr. St. Michael

Cambridge University

Review of this Book

We can say that the author is highly knowledgeable about what happened. This author described the subject matter of the book in a nice manner that tells us about the life of people from our past, their struggles as well as their sacrifice in five volumes.

The descriptions are brilliant, and the book gives within it's pages good information about the social things in the world. This book comes with a lot of parts and every part has a different meaning. The reader is able to grasp that the overall concept is truly unique. This author has made the subject matter very interesting, and we consider this to be fantastic reading. These 5 volumes are considered by us to be one of the best and factual series that have ever been seen or read.

C.N.E.W.—Dr. St. Michael

Cornerstone Fellowship Prison Ministry

348 N. Canyons Parkway

Livermore, CA 94551

January 27

Dr. St. Michael

Greetings Doc:

Please allow me to respond to your most recent letter. Pastor Becky has also received the letter and was impressed with your bio and also enjoyed your poems. And we all wish you luck in the poetry contest. Pastor Becky is the pastor for our Livermore campus, which is the largest of all the Cornerstone locations. She asked me to continue to communicate with you because her plate is very full as our lead pastor, and she prefers to let our Prison Ministry volunteers do the day-to-day work of corresponding with inmates.

You said in your recent letter how God speaks to you. This is a true blessing for mature Christians. It is almost beyond comprehension that the Creator of the universe, the Alpha and the Omega, our Lord and Savior, communicates with us. Of course, we know he is always there to listen to us through our prayers, but to have him respond in a discernable way, to hear his voice, is remarkable. Please consider the following verse, 1 Kings 19:11-13 when God speaks to Elijah:

"The Lord said, 'Go out and stand on the mountain in the presence of the Lord, of the Lord is about to pass by.' Then a great and powerful wind tore the mountains apart and shattered the rocks before the Lord, but the Lord was not in the wind. After the wind there was an earthquake, but the Lord was not in the Earthquake. After the earthquake came a fire, but the Lord was not in the fire. And after the fire came a gentle whisper. When Elija heard it, he pulled his cloak over his face and went out and stood at the mouth of the cave. Then a voice said to him, 'What are you doing here, Elijah?" (1 Kings 19:11-13 NIV).

C.N.E.W.—Dr. St. Michael

VOL. I

Table of contents

Table of contents for Books I-IV

In this book you will find precepts not known or taught today.

A. Preface

B. C.N.E.W: It's standard and what happens.

C. C.N.E.W: Beliefs

D. Biblical Battle Plan

- Who is C.N.E.W

- **<u>Supplement 1:</u>**

  ➢ Poems from Yehoshua

  ➢ Biography of Saint Michael

- **<u>Supplement 2:</u>**

  ➢ Congress declares Bible the Word of God

  ➢ Reading the levels of the Bible

  ➢ Pet Bird

  ➢ We can do for changes

- **Supplement 3**
  - ➢ The curses on America starting in 2016 to present
  - ➢ Vision again from Yehoshua
  - ➢ Parables to learn and to live by
- **Supplement 4: Historical and Theological Resources**
  - ➢ The coat of arms of Jesus Christ's Genealogy
  - ➢ Jewish Encyclopedia about Khazars.
  - ➢ Pilate's report to Tiberius Caesar of the arrest, trial, and crucifixion of Jesus Christ (Yehoshua).

C.N.E.W.—Dr. St. Michael

Table of Contents:

Supplement: 5

1. Body as the Temple of God
2. On the subject of human relationships
3. For your health and soul: The Bible and Health
4. Divine Diet
5. Junk food made me do it.
6. World's Healthiest diet
7. Are Vegetarians Healthier? Yes!
8. Protein
9. Eating for optimum Health
10. Nutrition through Macrobiotics
11. Swine as food
12. Cancer Cure
13. Common abbreviations for blood tests
14. Miscellaneous herbs for Health

Supplement: 6

A. Three separate creations

B. Superfetation

C. Seven deadly sins and Saligia

D. Christianity and Psychiatry

E. Jokes to laugh at or not?

Supplement: 7

1. San Quentin Prison, the Covid Pandemic, and deaths

2. Listing California facilities and Cal/pia

C.N.E.W.—Dr. St. Michael

NOTEBOOK: 2

TOPICAL CONTENTS:

Vol: II

A.

1. Christianity or Religious Tradition
2. The U.S. Constitution does not authorize any Government servant to appropriate even $1.00 of your money for charity to other persons or Nations.
3. America, A Christian Nation.
4. What is a Dollar?
5. Law of Grace: Conflict or Compliment
6. God (and Faith) of our Fathers.
7. Who has given America to the robbers and spoilers?
8. We must be Born Again.
9. Who are the Israelites?
10. Who are the Israelites today>
11. Could you be an Israelite and not know it?

12. Books by two Jewish scholars are awakening blinded Christians.

13. God's great race.

14. Suppose we are Israel (What difference does it make).

15. An open letter to any Minister who teaches "the Jews of Israel".

16. Which Bible and which version do you use?

17. Choosing a Bible.

18. The Marriage License, Issued by God, or the State?

19. Christianity – Religion of the West.

A. Statement by a fellow Minister, J.A. Weakley; to Dept of Corrections.

B. From: Restoration Bible Church; "Our Case".

C. From: C.N.E.W., "Statement of Beliefs".

NOTEBOOK: 3

TOPICAL CONTENTS

Vol: III

B.

1. Understanding Christianity's first Sacrament: The Four Modes of Baptism.

2. Old Testament Baptism.

3. New Testament Baptism.

4. Which Water saves?

5. Understanding Christ's mission and our message: What is the Gospel really?.

6. Understanding the biblical requirements for personal Salvation: What is Saving Faith?

7. Abrahamic Covenant: The Untold Story.

8. That familiar but so little understood subject: Our Sabbath-Ancient and Modern.

9. What the Bible Teaches about the Kingdom of God: The Everlasting Kingdom.

10. The Arminian view of the Devil.

11. Bible Prophecies and the European Peoples: The Gentiles in God's Plan.

12. A great voice from the past provides a clear warning for the present: Heresy defined.

13. The high cost of ignoring God's Laws.

14. For the benefit of our Pentecostal Brethren.

15. A keyword study leading to a greater bible understanding: A study into the meaning of the word "Gentile" as used in the Bible.

16. The meaning of the term "Religious Legalism": The Word of God dismantles a Religious Fence.

17. The mystery of the missing Bible Tribes: The real Diaspora.

18. A review of an important 1846 work authored by historian and theologian Dr. Moses Margoliouth: "The History of the Jews in Great Britain": Ancient Israel in Spain and Britain.

19. Ancient Hebrew sea Migrations.

20. The Hebrew-Celtic Connection

21. The Old Testament roots of Norse Mythology.

22. The Old Testament roots of Greek Mythology.

23. The Old Testament Roots of Celtic Mythology.

NOTEBOOK-4

TOPICAL CONTENTS:

VOL. IV

1. The Hebrew Foundation of Christ Church.
2. Did Israel Reject Christ.
3. Hebrew and English.
4. The other Exodus.
5. Lives of the Saints.
6. Capitalism in Bible Law and Prophecy.
7. The initial Evidence of the Holy Spirit.
8. Bible roots of the American Republic.
9. In the End, God: Guide to the study and interpretation of the Bible Prophecy.
10. The two houses of Israel.
11. The Seventy Weeks of Prophecy.
12. The year of Christ's Birth.
13. The United States in prophecy.
14. Tribulation or Rapture: Which?

15. Hell, and the after-death state.

16. The new Mythology of Afro-Centrism.

17. Why have the Jews not been able to fulfill most of the prophecies given to Israel?

18. Why is America Great?

19. What is the Kingdom of God?

20. How should we observe the Sabbath?

21. Seven uses of the Law of God.

22. The Ten Commandments from the New Testament.

23. Missing inheritors of the Covenant Promises.

24. Our Bible origins.

C.N.E.W.—Dr. St. Michael

NOTEBOOK-5

TOPICAL CONTENTS:

VOL. V

1. The lost chapter of Acts of the Apostles.

2. Lucifer: Angel of Light or Light Bearer and Son of Morning.

3. Angels: What you need to know.

4. Choosing a Bible.

5. Yah's Law.

6. Chart: Heritage of the Angle-Saxon Race

7. Chart: Christian Nations.

8. Three separate Creations.

9. Tribulation or Rapture: Which?

10. Secret Rapture.

11. History of the Christian Church.

12. Proof of the sexual seduction of Eve.

13. Doctrine of the Seedline Theory.

14. Websites on Arab and DNA similar to Jews.

15. Y-Chromosome evidence for a founder effect in Ashkenazi Jews.

16. Research papers proving two seedline seduction of Eve.

17. History of Lucifer.

C.N.E.W.—Dr. St. Michael

A. Preface

B. C.N.E.W: It's standard and What it represents.

C.N.E.W.—Dr. St. Michael

Preface

"C.N.E.W. Manual was designed to be informative and reliable. This manual's emphasis is on sharing and presenting the correct content and meaning of the Bible and history.

"C.N.E.W." is grateful to those who contributed, directly or indirectly in the compendium of this manual.

"C.N.E.W." believes that faith cometh by sharing the Word of God! Receive with meekness the engrafted word, which is able to save your soul.

We also thank God without ceasing, because when we received the Word of God, which we heard, we received it not as the Word of men, but, as it is in truth, the Word of God, which effectively worketh also in you that believes. For the Word of God is quick and powerful.

I warn you, fellow believers, that you must present your bodies as a living sacrifice that is Holy and acceptable to God. Rather be not conformed to this World; but be all of you transformed by the renewing of our minds, that we may prove what is the good, acceptable, and perfect will of God.

CHRISTIAN NATIONS * EAGLE WARRIORS

C.N.E.W.

1. Dr. St. Michael
   Executive President of C.N.E.W.
   Clergy Identification No: 10544; 7-7

   Executive Vice- President and Treasurer of C.N.E.W.

2. I.R.S., Church I.D. #EIN 33-06234 / 19 June
   Employ use and Church Account and donations, Mail

   Order/ For fund raising.

   Church by-laws and Postal Exempt #

3. **LOGO**

   Christian Nations-on top left side.
   Eagle Warriors-on the right side.
   With the Eagle in the center,
   C.N.E.W.: in block letters at the bottom and center.

   FLAG:

   a) C.N.E.W., in block letters (Red letters).

   b) Top half-White.

   c) Bottom half-Blue.

   d) Gold Rope and fringe around flag.

OUR STAND:

4. CHRISTIAN: One who professes belief in the teachings of Jesus Christ, in accord with the Bible. Acts 11:26; Rom. 10-17; 1 Tim. 1:14-17; 2 Tim. 3:15-17, 2:15.

NATIONS: A community of people that is composed of many nationalities and possessing a defined faith and government. Gen. 12:2-3; Isa. 11:12; John 10:16; Eph. 2:19; Phil. 3:20-21.

EAGLE: The seal and/or standard. Ex. 19:4; Isa. 40:31

WARRIORS: A person engaged in struggle for the Lord. Isa. 54:17; 2 Cor. 10:3-5; Eph. 6:10-18; 2 Tim. 2:1-4.

C.N.E.W.—Dr. St. Michael

Copyright 2025: C.N.E.W. : All rights reserved

We are happy to grant permission for items in the "Bible" section to be reproduced in their entirety, as long as the following stipulations are observed:

(1) C.N.E.W. must be designated as the original publisher;

(2) The specific C.N.E.W. website must be noted;

(3) The author's name must remain attached to the materials;

(4) Any references, footnotes, or endnotes that accompany the article must be included with any written reproduction of the article;

(5) Alterations of any kind are strictly forbidden (e.g., photographs, charts, graphics, quotations, etc., must be reproduced exactly as they appear in the original;

(6) Serialization of written material (e.g., running an article in several parts) is permitted, as long as the whole of the material is made available, without editing, in a reasonable length of time;

(7) Articles, in whole or in part, may not be offered for sale or included in items offered for sale; and

(8) Articles may be reproduced in electronic form for posting on Websites provided that they are not edited or altered from their original content and that credit is given to C.N.E.W., including the web location from which the ARTICLES WERE TAKEN.

For catalog, samples, or further information, contact: ON WEBSITE.

1. C.N.E.W., Business and Resources Manual
2. What the Logo means, the flag, and beliefs.
3. **Index:** See Website: What is offered; Forms and Membership.
4. How and what to do when starting a business and/or a non-profit business.
5. Where to write or call; A-Z on resources:
6. Marriage Laws of all 50 States.
7. Laws for Ministers: See Family Law in your State.

5. All donations, up to 50% of income is tax-exempt. Fund raising activity by members is tax exempt, by donating their services to their church. Passive investments are tax exempt.

6. California Marriage Laws: Civil Code. §4213-4215. Marriage License from County Clerk's Office, the fee's may vary…

7. Exempted from licensing requirements to perform psychological and psychometric services or counseling.

8. Discrimination against a Prisoner Inmate Minister is Illegal under Title 3 of Civil 3 of Civil Rights Act of 1994, 42 U.S.C.A §2000b.

9. Religious Counseling; Exempt from License. California Bus & Pro. Code. sec. §171881; sec. §2908.

SEE WEBSITE

1. **EPISTEMOLOGY:**

a. Epistemology means the study of knowledge.

b. How do we know what we know?

c. The Christian Philosophy of knowledge.

2. Christian teachings established firmly upon philosophy and thoroughly historical apologetics.

a. Facts implicate ultimate authority (Yehovah).

3. **History of the Tribes of Israel**

a. Parthian elites that chose Parthia's Emperors were called the "Magi" or "Wise Men."

b. These Parthian officials worshipped Jesus Christ. (Yehoshua).

C.N.E.W-BELIEFS

1. **GOD:** Most Christians are Orthodox on this teaching. Believing in the (3) three in One (Father, Son, and Holy Spirit). There are heresies within the Church. Some teach one or more of the following:

   a. That Jesus Christ is the Son of God, but not God the Son.

   b. That there is no Trinity.

   c. That the Holy Spirit is not a person but only an influence or something else.

2. **SALVATION:** Most Christians are orthodox on this teaching, believing that Salvation come's by faith in the Lord Jesus Christ.

   a. Most are Calvinistic by believing that God chooses some to be saved and others to be lost.

   b. There are many who are still holding to the Arminian point of view that man has free will and can be saved when they choose.

3. **WE ARE ISRAEL:** This is a point of view that all or most agree on. America believes that we are Israel today. This can be taken in one or two separate ways of both views together.

    1. **PHYSICAL ISRAEL:** Most people believe that the Americans and related people are the physical descendants of the lost tribes of the Bible who are recorded as being taken captive by Assyria and the Parthian Empire's,(2-Kings 17:6-8; 18:13). In the Old and New Testaments and acknowledged as being scattered,(Isa.26:15; 27:6; 42:16-19; 43:10-21; Hosa.1:10-11; Matt.10:6; 15:24; James 1:1).

    2. **SPIRITUAL ISRAEL:** Most are split on this point. This is the orthodox teaching of Protestant Churches.

a. Born-again believers are now Israel. Many hold both of these views together.

b. That we are physical descendants of Israel in the Old Testament.

c. That spiritual Israel is also born-again. This may explain Romans 9:6: "For they are not all spiritual Israel, which are of physical Israel." Some hold to one or both of these beliefs.

4. **GOD'S LAWS:** Most believe that God's (Yahweh) laws of the Old Testament apply to us today, (Matthew 5:17-19).

1. **CLEAN FOOD LAWS:** Food laws were not annulled in the New Testament, and still remain, (Lev. 11; Acts 10:14-28). This is the historic orthodox teaching of the early Christian Church. To name a people who this believe is or was held by:

a. Irenaeus **b.** William Tyndale **c.** John Calvin **d.** Martin Luther **e.** Matthew Henry **f.** C.H. Spurgeon **g.** D.L. Moody. There are only a few people that do not hold this view.
2. This is a major conflict with today's churches because they teach against God's (Yahweh) law.
   a. Teaching that God's (Yahweh) laws are done away with and no longer apply to them.
   b. This teaching in our Bibles calls it, "Iniquity", (Matt. 7:21-23; Rom. 6:19; Titus 2:7). Thus, it is clear that modern Christians are in terrible error because they serve God (Yahweh) in their own way and not according to Scripture. This rebellion today by modern churches shows that they are attempting to make themselves God by rejecting the laws and making their own laws.
5. **RELIGIONS:** Most believe that other religions are a damnable religion because they reject our Savior

and their adherents attack and blaspheme our Savior. Jesus Christ (Yehoshua) no doubt had the same opinion of these religions, (Matt. 23:15, Luke 20:24-27; Rev. 2:9; 3:9).

6. **THE JEWS (as a race):** This is a hot subject with much discussion surrounding it and there is no majority opinion on this subject. It is agreed that most of todays Jews are not related to the Jews of the Bible.

   a. Today's Eastern European Jews (Ashkenazim) are the descendants of the Khazars (Khazars) who are of Turkish/Mongolian lineage. They are not semitic. They are called Jews today because they converted to Judaism, and this is explained as such in the most Standard and Jewish Encyclopedia. These Khazar Jews make up 85-90% of todays Jews. They claim to be physical Jews but, in fact, they are only Jews by religious belief and have no way to substantiate their lineage. The Bible speaks of this and calls them the synagogue of Satan.

b. We next have the Sephardic Jews, which make up about 10-15% of todays Jews. They can trace their lineage back to the time of the New Testament. This makes the Sephardic Jews from the Southern Kingdom of Judah of the Old Testament while the other half are converts to Judaism as shown in Esther 8:17 as well as, "The works of Josephus, ant. Book 13, Chapter 9, sec. 1". Most converts were Edomites (descendants of Esau and sometimes called Idumeans, (The Red Lineage in History). As to this writer's lineage, I am from the Tribe of Gad.

c. There is a belief by some that todays Jews are the physical descendants of Satan. They believe that Satan had sex with Eve, which produced Cain who produced the Canaanites who eventually produced todays Jews. Some hold that Cain and Able were twins, and Cain was fathered by Satan and Able by Adam. This view is heled by 1/3. This is no doubt one of the views of the Seedline beliefs which gets more attention than any of the other beliefs.

d. The question of the Jews as a race is a complex issue. This complex issue is something we can oppose together. The Bible teaches that all chosen people are children of faith, (Gal. 3:7).

    e. We find these modern churches to be of double mindedness because most of the teachings today lack spiritual discernment.

7. **RAPTURE:** Most Christians are Historic Futurists, and believe that Christians will go through the Tribulation, after which time, Jesus Christ will return. The Battle of Armageddon occurs, and Jesus Christ then sets up his physical Kingdom on Earth. There are some who hold to Dispensationalism, with pre- and Mid-Tribulation, and Rapture Beliefs; In Gr. Harpaso, meaning to carry off; Grasp Hastily; Snatch up; to seize and overcome; to plunder. There are also Preterists within the church as well. There are some who are convinced that there will be no rapture before the Tribulation. This belief comes from J.N. Darby (1830) and is a view that is not found in scriptures that the secret rapture teaching contradicts, (Matt. 13; Rev. 19).

8. Christianity is already a recognized faith, and most Judeo-Christians classify this.
    1. The Kingdom of Cults by Walter Martin;
    2. Thru the Bible with J. Vernon McGee by J. Vernon McGee; Vol. 5;
    3. What the Cults Believe by Irvine Robertson (stating Today's Christianity is not a cult as are the other systems are considered. It is rather a theory that countries are the ten-tribes of Israel.)
    4. The Chaos of Cults by Jan Karel Van Baalen;
    5. The Dake's Annotated Reference Bible (KJV) by F.J. Dake;
    6. These Christian authors recognize that Christians exist, even though they do not agree with all of Christianity's teachings. The U.S. Department of Treasure (IRS) and the Churches, and the National Counsil of Churches each recognize Christianity as a Church

denomination today and will continue to hold and practice our faith as best as we can.

C.N.E.W.—Dr. St. Michael

A BIBLICAL BATTLE PLAN

A BIBLICAL BATTLE PLAN:

Christians fighting the culture wars do not have to enter the fray without having a plan. Yet, according to some field reports, too often, that is what happens. Believers fight spiritual battles with carnal weapons and temporal strategies. "The Devil's real busy trying to keep us away from what works and gets us all involved in what doesn't work." So, what is the biblical battle plan? Here are a few of the scripture passages most often mentioned by those on the front lines:

1. KNOW YOUR ORDERS: Jesus Christ (Yahshua), commissioned his army of followers with specific instructions: To introduce Him to the whole world (Matt. 28:19). Other things, from eradicating abortion to preventing prostitution are fine tactics as long as they advance the overall strategy of getting the gospel message out.

2. **FOLLOW YOUR LEADER:** Jesus Christ (Yahshua), the Captain of our faith, was certainly more gravely mistreated than any of his American followers have ever been. Peter tells us that Jesus Christ (Yahshua), set the example for us, and that we should follow in His steps, "Being reviled, He did not revile in return; while suffering, he uttered no threats, but kept entrusting himself to him who judges righteously," (1 Peter 2:21-23).

3. **LOVE YOUR ENEMY:** And that is just the beginning. According to Luke 6:27-30: "Do good to those who hate you, bless those who curse you, pray for those who mistreat you. If someone strikes you on one cheek, turn to him the other also…and if anyone takes what belongs to you, do not demand it back." That kind of love is bound to get noticed! No wonder Jesus Christ (Yahshua) said, "By this all

men will know that you are my disciples, if you love one another," (John 13:35).

4. WATCH YOUR SPEECH: "For out of the overflow of the heart the mouth speaks," according to Matthew 12:34. What does that say about people who carry hate filled placards? Paul's communication guidelines are: "Let your conversation be always full of grace, seasoned with salt, so that you may know how to answer everyone," (Col. 4:6). Salt certainly is needed to hold back corruption, but a good dose of graciousness can help to soothe the sting. Besides, Solomon says, angry words are self-defeating: "A gentle answer turns away wrath, but a harsh word stirs up anger," (Prov. 15:1). It is true that Christ sometimes used harsh words ("Whitewashed tombs," "Brood of vipers,"), but they were reserved for false religious leaders whose teachings were

blinding sinners to the truth. Contrast that with Jesus' words to Pilate, the representative of the corrupt Roman government (John 18:19) or to the debauched woman at the well, (John 4).

5. WATCH YOUR BACK: While you are busy making a frontal attack on society's evils, Satan may be attacking you from behind. "See to it," says the writer of Hebrews, "that no bitter root grows up to cause trouble and defile many," (Heb. 12:15). Bitterness is a common wound in the culture wars, and it is often fatal to an effective Christian testimony.

BEFORE YOU RESPOND

For Christians in the United States who love their country, evidence of its moral decline is easy to spot. There is the brothel on Main street and the abortionists clinic on elm. God is banned from public schools but everyone else from Marx to Mapplethorpe seems welcome. Homosexuals push their lifestyle while Hollywood pushes the limits.

What often gets lost in the rhetoric as Christians respond, however, is the personal needs behind our opponent's political stance. As the director of the Christian Embassy says, "Not everyone has our biblical background. As people come to know Christ in a personal way, there are political and moral convictions that follow. But you cannot assume that a person who does not have a personal relationship with Christ is going to share your convictions."

Based on the experience of believers whose ministry is interaction with groups and individuals widely considered, "the enemy," here are some tips for pointing people to Christ, rather than just making a point:

1. **<u>GET GROUNDED IN THE WORD:</u>** The Bible has much to say about the Christian's reaction to a secular society. Without a firm grasp of these principles, believers tend to simply mimic the

methods of the world. Most of the time, such methods are based on emotion (what feels good) or expedience (what seems to work). Thus, angered Christians rant and rave because it makes them feel better or they engage in peaceful resistance because it worked for the civil rights movement. "But we shouldn't take our cues from the ACLU or People of the American Way," the director of the Center for Law and Religious Freedom in Annadale stated, "We don't use the rules they play by. We're called to be different.

2. **<u>PRAY FOR YOUR ENEMIES:</u>** "First thing every morning, we read the scriptures and pray for those closest to us, then we pray for the wider needs of a greater spiritual family and of the country and the world. We believe prayer is the key to loving Jesus Christ (Yahshua) loved. How can you love somebody who hates you? You can't, until Jesus

Christ (Yahshua), gives you the same heart for them that he has for you. That's not anything you can study or take a course for. You can't microwave your spiritual life; this is a gourmet dinner, and it takes time." The Master media International Group tries to make it easy for believers to pray for their "enemies" in Hollywood. Every year, the organization distributes 40,000 copies of the "Media Leader Prayer Calendar," a day-by-day listing of the most influential executives in the entertainment industry. Concerned Christians may eventually feel compelled to write protest letters to some of those executives, but at least they will have first prayed for them by name. (To get a free copy of the prayer calendar, plus a complimentary subscription to The Mediator newsletter, call 1-800-447-8711).

3. **GET TO KNOW YOUR OPPONENTS PERSONALITY:** "Sometimes, Christians make outlandish statements in the media without having researched it or having even spoken to that individual." The Christian Embassy organization seeks to make personal contact with politicians from across the philosophical spectrum and to avoid play politics. Building bridges to a pro-abortion or pro-homosexual politician does not always come naturally. "It's difficult because each of us in our own hearts has political convictions. But our desire is to work with people of all backgrounds, all sociological and ethnic persuasions. If we are going to work effectively in terms of evangelism and discipleship, we do not have the privilege of remaining aloof from those we disagree with."

4. **LOOK AT ALL YOUR OPTIONS:** "The first question we as should be, 'What means are

available to further righteousness without repudiating Christian Love? If you get the first at the expense of the second, you've failed." Often, this means looking beyond the first reaction that springs to mind.

When the traveling production of Jesus Christ, Superstar made a stop recently in Greenville, S.C., conservative Christians were in an uproar. Pastors from nearly 40 churches got together several months in advance to coordinate their response. Early suggestions were predicable. Some wanted to picket, others wanted to sing and preach outside of the theater. Another group wanted to pressure the city council to ban the show. But the more they debated, the less appealing all of the options looked.

Pastor Al McClaran of Morningside Baptist Church saw the show as an "opportunity to present Jesus Christ (Yahshua), to our community in a positive way. "We wanted to make Jesus Christ (Yahshua), not the superstar."

Toward the end, the group decided on a media campaign designed not necessarily to keep people away from the show, but to make them think about the identity of Jesus Christ (Yahshua). They rented billboards and designed a message proclaiming Jesus Christ (Yahshua), Savior, Jesus Christ, Superstar—They are Not the Same." Then, on the weekend of the shows run, they took out full page newspaper ads contrasting quotes from the musical ("He's just a man,") with quotes from the Bible ("I and the Father are one".) Bible verses were carefully selected to not only refute the show's blasphemies, but more importantly, to present the plan of Salvation.

Pastor Al McClaran and his colleagues were pleased with the results. "If people think we're a bunch of foaming at the mouth radicals, it just turns them off. I think the positive approach has done a whole lot more good than any other approach has managed to do. Even if people go on and see the show, they have it in the back of their mind that this isn't the Jesus Christ (Yahshua), of the Bible, then we've succeeded."

Of all the commands in Scripture, Jesus Christ (Yahshua), said two matter the most! Twice in the ministry of Jesus Christ (Yahshua), men interrupted him with questions about the ultimate priorities in life. In Matthew 22:40, Jesus Christ (Yahshua), said and it's still true today, "All the Law and Prophets hang on these two commandments." Both of the answers were the same, "Love the Lord your God(Yahweh), with all your being and love your neighbor as yourself."

As a Christian, this is your most important priority!

WHO'S

CHRISTIAN NATIONS-EAGLE WARRIORS

SUPPLEMENTS: 1-10; TO ENCOURAGE YOU TO

SHARE MORE.

A. Poems from Yehoshua.

B. Bio of St. Michael

C. Curses on America—2016

D. Parables in the Gospels: 39

SUPPLEMENTS: 1-16

You do the research, some of this may assist you.

A. How to become a Christian.

B. Bill of Rights + Declaration of Independence

C. Poems from Yehoshua

D. Bio – St. Michael

A. How to become a Christian:

The Bible say's God loved the world so much that HE GAVE HIS ONLY BEGOTTEN SON. THAT WHO EVER BELIEVES IN HIM WILL NOT PERISH BUT HAVE EVERLASTING LIFE (John 3:16). God loves you and wants to have a relationship with you.

1. All of us have sinned and come short of the glory of God, (Rom. 3:23;6:23; 1 John 1:10).
2. Believe in the Lord Jesus Christ and you will be saved, (Acts 16:31; John 1:12).
3. If you confess with your mouth the Lord Jesus Christ and believe in your heart that God raised Jesus Christ from the dead, you will be saved, (Rom.10:9; Eph. 2:8-9).

B. U.S. CONSTITUTION: Bill of Rights: Article 1. Declaration of Independence.

That all people are equal among human beings.

No one that exists is superior nor inferior.

We should easily express how great a mirror of friendship and how great an image of a loving society reflects. We display our attachments in actions and sounds together, in enjoying one another's company and pleasure and relish friendship.

What forest produces only one tree of a single species? We are many trees together, who express and display a communion in various classes to multiply our joy as one host of humans. This is what being Christian and American is about.

C. I freely admit (Yehoshua) has redeemed me and has been merciful TO ME THROUGH Jesus Christ. My Lord Jesus Christ, (Yehoshua) has brought me to the true faith, (Heb. 4:8). It's my prayer this will clear up any misunderstanding of scriptures and our Belief's.

C.N.E.W.—Dr. St. Michael

Little Puppy

by: Dr. St. Michael

I am that little puppy in the window,
I know you care because you just stand there and stare.
You take me home and wash me
and love and care for me.
Sometimes, I do things wrong, but that's ok!
Because you still love and hug me because,
I am the little puppy that loves you too!
Now, I ask why can't all of you Brothers and
Sisters do the same thing, as you do me,
after all,
I am just that little puppy that
Loves you too!

THE BUTTERFLY

By: Dr. St. Michael

I am the Butterfly that passes by your window.
As I go by seeing all beautiful humans look at me in amazement.
They wonder how I fly so easily in the air.
It's part of God's Spirit that keeps me adrift.
Then I wonder why can't those human's completely trust God in everything, as I do.
He gives me Air, Light, and Food.
But most of all his love for me and other's.
As I show I am his beautiful creation that really loves all of you too…
So, I ask, can you show God's love to others as he does for you.
'Love', is the greatest gift of all.
So, share it…

C.N.E.W.—Dr. St. Michael

FISH AT BOTTOM OF THE SEA

I am the fish at the bottom of the sea.
You can't see me, yet I am down here.
Just like God and the Spirit, you can't see them.
Yet, you know they're watching everything you do,
because their right next to you…
You HAVE FREE WILL TO DO WHAT YOU CHOOSE.
You know they love you, so what you going to do.
Everything that's on Earth, they did for you.
So, what are you going to do for them, in taking
care of this Earth and other's.
If you really care, you can show them your love for
everything.
I am the fish at bottom of the sea and pray you don't eat
me…
Your love for me and others, you show your actions in love.

C.N.E.W.—Dr. St. Michael

FIND 30 BOOKS OF THE BIBLE

The names of 30 books of the Bible are in this paragraph. Can you find them? This is a most remarkable puzzle. It was found by a gentleman in an airplane seat pocket on a flight from Los Angeles to Honolulu, keeping him occupied for hours. He enjoyed it so much he passed it on to some friends. One friend from Illinois worked on this while fishing from his john boat.

Another friend studied it while playing his banjo. Elaine Taylor, a columnist friend was so intrigued by it that she mentioned it in her weekly newspaper column. Another friend judges the job of solving this puzzle so involved that she brews herself a cup of tea to help her nerves.

There will be some names that are really easy to spot. That is a fact. Some people, however, will soon find themselves in a jam, especially since the book names are not necessarily capitalized. Truthfully, from answers we get, we are forced to admit that it usually takes a Minister or Scholar to see some of them at the worst.

Research has shown that something in our genes is responsible for the difficulty we have in seeing the books in this paragraph. During a recent fund-raising event, which featured this puzzle, the Alpha Delta Phi lemonade booth set a new sales record. The local paper, The Chronicle, surveyed over 200 patrons who reported that this puzzle was one of the most difficult they had ever seen.

As Daniel Humana humbly puts it, the books are all right there in plain view, hidden from sight. Those able to find them will hear lamentations from those who have to be shown. One revelation that may help is that books like Timothy and Samuel may occur without their numbers.

Also, keep in mind that spaces and punctuation in the middle of words are normal. A chipped attitude will help you compete really well against those who claim to know the answers. Remember, there is no need for a mad exodus, there really are 30 books of the Bible lurking somewhere in the paragraph waiting to be found.

TWINKLE-TWINKLE

By Dr. St. Michael

I am the star that looks so far.

I've always been here, adrift in space where time does not exist.

Yet, God placed me here to watch over you.

Do you know who I am yet?

I was there watching when Jesus Christ was born,

and when He was nailed to the cross for you.

Because of God's love for you, I'll be watching over you, until you come

home…

I am one of God's messengers, sent to tell you that Jesus Christ loves you

so much, no matter what you do.

I'll be watching over you.

My hope is that someday, you'll share Jesus Christ's gift of love for the

earth and others,

by sharing His love in all you do.

IT'S ABOUT TIME AND OUTERSPACE

By: Dr. St. Michael

You may wonder what am I doing in this place,

in all the Universe, you may wonder, I can't be the only one

in this little place called Earth.

Did you know there's others out there.

You're never alone in Universe.

God put you in this little place you know for a reason.

Each of you may not realize that I've a plan just for you…

I am like the wind; you don't understand where I am from

or where I am going.

I speak to each of you, and you don't realize I am

right next to you…

You just have to ask and listen and you'll

hear me as your guide.

You ever wonder about the voice you hear in your head? It's me…

I want all of you to love each other and take care of your Earth.

When is the last time you told someone that you love them

and really meant it…

After all, love is what keeps all of you alive.

So, reach out today and tell someone you love them as I do you…

C.N.E.W.—Dr. St. Michael

WATER—WATER AND NO PLACE TO GO

By: Dr. St. Michael

Water—Water all around me as I stay afloat in my little rowboat.

I am in this huge sea and don't know which direction to go.

As I lay half asleep, a voice comes to me saying, "when it's

night, follow the brightest star in the North, it will lead

you in the right direction.

Just like my word.

I am always watching over you, because I am God,

who created you and loved you.

I've given you (2) two hands to paddle, so use them.

When you get home, read my word, it's truth and

your guide for you because I love you…

So, when you have problems, pray to me, and read my

guide,

I'll be listening and watching you until you come home.

I love you and all my creations.

Teach others love because it's what keeps all of you alive.

BUMBLEBEE BUMBLEBEE

By: Dr. St. Michael

I am as fast as can be, you can't catch me.

Because I am a Bumblebee.

That's why I am so happy, it's not all about little me.

Seeing all the beautiful things God made for you and me.

Seeing humans destroying the flowers and water, we drink

and changing the landscape.

All this I don't like because someday you'll be killing little me.

That's okay because I still love you my friends.

No matter what you do to me.

Jesus Christ loves us all equally and I love you too…

Maybe someday you'll stop killing my friends, and start loving everything, including me and others.

Once you do this, all will be happy.

"Love" is what keeps us alive longer.

Let your actions show Jesus Christ's love through you.

After all, I am just a little Bumblebee, so please love me.

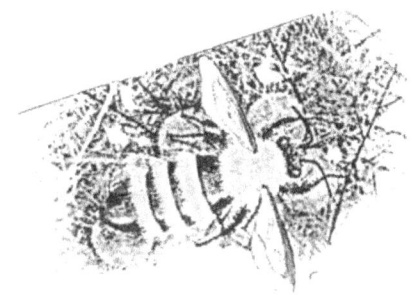

BLUE SEA

By: Dr. St. Michael

All around me as far as I can see is Blue sea.

As I set in this blue sea and realizing it's

you Lord around me. "Lord, help me."

My Lord answers. "It's about time you called to me,

I've been here all the time waiting for you to call me

for help if you'll listen.

It's because 'I love you', I am here, so let me guide you.

Someday, you'll come home and be rewarded for what

you have

done for me.

That Blue Sea all around you is my love.

You must show love to others in all you do,

because it's not about you.

I want you to walk to strangers, take their hand and hug

them.

It's from you and the Lord.

Because of my love, you must also share this love with others."

THIS IS WHAT BEING A FOLLOWER IS ALL ABOUT.

TIGER IN A CAGE

By: Dr. St. Michael

I am a tiger in the zoo,

I am looking at you.

Do you know what I see?

People, people looking at me.

Throw scraps at me, what I'd

really like to eat is you,

so why do you do this to me,

when all I want is to be free?

I am one of God's creatures who wants

to be free.

My kind used to run from sea to sea.

God created me for your pleasure,

so, God created you and me so

we could be friends.

God says we're to love all of you,

no matter what you do to us.

C.N.E.W.—Dr. St. Michael

If this is true, then show God's love

to me and set me free.

Remember, God loves you and me,

so, can we show God's love to others?

You know "Love," is the key that makes us all happy…

EXHIBITS IN SUPPORT:

SUMMARY OF MY LIFE (BIO):

By: Dr. St. Michael

A. Reflecting on life changing events.

B. Resume of what I've done in the past, and the changes from God since coming to Prison.

C. The articles that I've written to teach others the truth!

D. Medical issues and what transpired in my life.

C.N.E.W.—Dr. St. Michael

FROM: Dr. St. Michael

IN RE; Reflecting on Life Changing Events.

I currently have a lot of time to reflect on my life. Since coming to prison, I have completely changed my life through accepting the Lord Jesus Christ as my savior and walking with Him now on a daily basis through my prayers. I believe Jesus Christ offers us all hope, healing, and a new purpose for each ones life.

Through my amazing awakening to my new hope and my life's purpose, I am called to serve my neighbor and to replace the cycle of my life of crime with a cycle of renewal and giving back to my community rather than taking away, as I did in my past.

Since becoming a follower of my beliefs, I have seen the errors of my past mistakes and I have spent my prison sentence studying, attending church regularly, teaching, and helping other inmates and staff better understand what the Word is teaching, and as you can see from all the degrees I have obtained, I have been attending school. I do this so that I can be a model and teach others the truth!

My purpose for this letter is to bring a worthy need to your attention. I have decided that it is in my heart to serve my Lord and others in what every capacity he uses me in, but in order to do this, I need your assistance, which is necessary to get me out the door so that I can.

To do as my Lord commands of me, I need to go through all the land preaching the Kingdom of Heaven and to heal all people of sickness who receive Christ and repent. To prepare His people for His imminent return. I can understand any reservation you may have, but please know that I am sincere in what I have to do now. I am only requesting that you, if the Lord moves you, to assist me in this endeavor, so that I can do what the Lord has told me to accomplish for him.

In sharing the following comments from the school:

A. "It is quite obvious that you have the gifts of exhortation, and this helps. Coupled with great organization (neatness) skills, way to go."

B. This was well written and highly devotional from your end. Your insights into the patriarchs are good and your report profiles were good except a bit short which is why you received an A- rather than A or A+. Keeping the Word of God elevated to the level you take it bodes well for a spirit filled teacher of the Word like you aspire to. All in all, an exceptional paper.

C. Brother St. Michael, you have really developed in your analyses of your studies. Your thoughts on this were very good, profound, and devotional. The miracles were wonderfully presented, and I sure loved your thoughts on how the elitists have hijacked our schools in order to make converts to their immoral, anti-Christian ideals. Bingo, bro!!! As I read over these words, I was drawn to God by the words of a man who is deeply committed to Him in every way. I hope you are as pleased with your work as I am my friend.

D. Your work exceeds the norm, Doc. Even the ancillary documents were all submitted with perfection. The information you present is great reading for Christians of all ages; especially the historical edge you bring to it. Frankly, this reads like a Bible handbook. The Perils of Prodigals—superbly done. I know, without question, that God is using you for His glory. Keep these things in your heart to use forever, my friend. In short, I am privileged to be your mentor and friend, and look forward to working with you wherever you are, inside or outside Doc. Faithful men of God like you are rare. May your tribe increase, my dear brother.

E. My dear brother Doc, your work is becoming increasingly blessed. Insights are great, and I loved your insightful commentary. Good work my friend. Your work continues to be exceptionally well written and presented. It is obvious that you pay particular attention to the authority of the Word while doing more than giving mere lip service to our Lord and Savior Jesus Christ. I am proud of you as a student Doc!

F. Doc, your course work continues in the path of excellence. Great insights and applications which I agree, are life changing albeit, missing elements in much of the preaching today. The truths you bring forth are always very enlightening. Glad to see another w ho loves the Word as much as I do. I am impressed brother.

G. Superb work, Doc. Praise Jesus!!! I am still amazed by the conviction by which you present your ideas.

Good going. Whenever you approach the Word of God as the inerrant will of the Master, it is noteworthy! Very thorough and well thought out. Excellent thoughts in your summary as you applied this to our Spanish speaking breather. I just finished praying for you. May the Lord Jesus Christ reveal Himself to you fresh today, my friend.

I learned, in my studies of Epistemology, to establish firmly upon Christian philosophy and thoroughly consider the historical apologetics. These facts implicate the ultimate authority. The Parthian elites that chose Parthian Emperors were called the "Magi" or "Wise men", and these officials worshipped our Lord Jesus Christ.

My prayerful hope is that you have it in your heart to help me. I want so badly to be the tool that the Lord wants me to be. Even the saints in the early apostolic church needed the aid of their better positions brothers and sisters. Like them, I am also in need of your assistance.

I humbly present my request to you so that I can one day very soon stand proud and boldly proclaim the truth of my Lord's soon coming Kingdom. Your act of faith in me could potentially reach countless souls, reaping a bountiful harvest for both of us in the world. At the very least, please pray about this.

I thank you in advance for your consideration of my matter.

May the Lord continue to bless an

enrich you as you labor for Him…

Sincerely, In my master's Service…

Dr. St. Michael

"For we are his workmanship, created in Christ Jesus for good works, which God prepared beforehand, that we should walk in them," (Ephesians 2:10).

Permit me to paint a word picture to illustrate how this works. Imagine for a moment that you are observing the Lord in Heaven with an entourage of Angelic beings following behind and embracing every word and gesture from the Master.

They all walk down the golden street and have traveled a considerable distance when my master stops at the window of a celestial jewelry store. There among the jewels and finery, is a huge diamond, glistening silently in the brilliance of His light.

The entourage gasps at the beauty they behold there in the store window.

Then the Lord says, "You might not realize it, but this is St. Michael. When I first called him, he was a worthless chunk of coal. He was a mess of coal dust, dirt, and impurity. Look at him now, isn't St. Michael beautiful? He didn't get that way by himself, however. It took a lot of work and skilled workmanship to make what he is today."

"Praise your holy name," Comes the whisper of astonishment from the gallery.

The master continues, "It took an infinite amount of pressure and friction to make something beautiful out of that old chunk of coal. I had to chip away all the waste and worthlessness he represented. I spent much of his life polishing and refining old St. Michael, but I think you will agree that it was worth all the effort."

The gallery nods as one and buzzes with excitement over what God can do to make something beautiful out of what is otherwise ugly.

He is the God of Grace, Love, and Justice after all.

I do not wish to depreciate the redemptive plan of God because I recognize it's vast importance, and that the redemptive program serves to bring glory and honor to His name. The Angels in Heaven rejoice and glorify the Lord when a soul on Earth experiences redemption.

C.N.E.W.—Dr. St. Michael

Now on this issue, I'd like to share my recent medical history.

On 28 March to 1 April 2015, this is what transpired:

A. At 4 P.M., or Count time, I started to throw up blood, and my cell mate kind of panicked. I told him not to worry, "I got this." As C/O Ms. Islas was walking the tier for Count, she stopped at my door and saw that the front of my t-shirt and shorts were covered in blood. C/O Ms. Islas had the tower Officer (Building control) open my cell door. Then a medical staff member who C/O Ms. Islas called, brought in a wheelchair. I told them that I could walk, and they said that it was the only way to get me to medical before the count cleared. The "LVN", did my vitals and called the Doctor.

The Doctor ordered me to be taken to the hospital. The Doctor also had C/O R. Wynn sign for and get my prescriptions to take with us to the hospital. As we entered "San Joaquin General Hospital" in French Camp, California, I grabbed the green bag from under C/O R. Wynn's arm and then I just kept throwing up blood.

When I was done, I measured it and it went to my 2nd knuckle on my index finger. I was then rushed to the intensive care unit where the Nurse asked me if I had had this procedure done before. I told her that I was the last of 10 before, and 9 had lowers done and I was the only one getting an upper. I asked her if they could wipe the tube off first because last time it left a funny taste in my mouth.

All of the staff in the room began laughing and explaining that the same tube would be getting used on multiple people. I promised that I already knew that. After a while, I asked if I could go to the restroom, and I did not make it because there was blood leaking from my rear, and I put a lot in the plastic bag stool. After the nurse hooked me up to the monitor, I kept telling the nurse that her machine was broken. She told me that it was not broken and that it was all new and state of the art.

I repeated myself, saying, "Look, your machine is not working. It's going 'eeeee." I heard someone say, "Code Blue in ICU," just before I passed out. This happened to me twice. When I woke up, I said, "Well, I see I'm not going any were."

B. Then I heard someone telling me to talk to the Chaplain David Staggs and to explain to him about his problems and for him not to worry about them because the Lord has it handled. He would be blessed if he listened to what was said, and if not…then not…

So, after all of this, I returned to the facility. On Easter Sunday, I went to talk to Chaplain Skaggs and to explain to him what had happened to me. His response was that he did not have the time and it could not be done.

So, I left, and then walked around the track and prayed about this. "Lord, you need to do something about this if you want me to do this. I saw Satan was fighting to stop this." So, I walked back into the Chapel and said, "Lord, this in Your hands!" A few minutes later, the lights in the whole prison went out, so the Guards came in and told everyone they had to leave. I told everyone to meet by the bench in the yard.

So, Mr. David Skaggs, the Head of all "C.D.C.R.," came out with his wife. I again told him who I am and that I had a message for him that needed to be given. He refused. So, he started to preach again, and I prayed for the Lord to deal with him. After a few minutes, the whole prison was in a complete black out. We were all called back in to lock up due to the power outage (not sure why the back up generators did not work). The whole area around the prison also had no power. (God did this).

So, I sent this to Mr. David Skaggs at C.D.C.R., Sac-Office where he turned it over to Custody-Staff.

C. As to my health, I have been cured of Hepatitis C. Dr. Horowitz stated, "Currently, your diagnosis included bleeding, esophageal varices, (ESLD) End Stage Liver Disease, and a lowered platelet count. Your high-risk status is determined by your Medical conditions. Ultra-sound found few Gallstones, Cirrhosis & Fibrosis, Enlarged Spleen."

D. Looking at it this way…The Lord will keep me alive until I've accomplished what He wants me to do!

C.N.E.W.—Dr. St. Michael

NAME: St. Michael

INMATE#: B-78150

Listed are changes made through Rehab in Prison:

1. 1995-1999: Library Assistant. (Calipatria, California).

    a. Completed Lawyer's Assistant Course's Training for Non-Attorney.

    b. Associate degree in Judicial Science (G.P.A-4.0).

2. 2004: Building Maintenance (Corcoran, California).

3. 2005: Graphic Arts (Corcoran, California).

4. 2010: master's degree in counseling

5. 2010: Doctorate degree

    a. 2016: 6 units from 2nd doctoral degree.

    b. GPA 4.0 (A & A+).

6. 1999: Saved the life of one of the staff (K. Sparks LTA 1): St. Michael had stayed at work after his co-workers left. He was doing research at his desk. He

looked up and saw K. Sparks was not at his desk. St. Michael decided to check on K. Sparks and found him on the floor. St. Michael found that K. Sparks had a weak pulse, so he ran to the front door and beat on the window to get the C/O's attention. St. Michael informed the C/O of what was going on and the C/O then ran to get someone from medical. St. Michael went back to attend to K. Sparks until medical staff arrived and took K. Sparks to the hospital. The Captain told St. Michael, "Good think you were there. He could have laid there all night."

7. 31 May 2017: C/O Armeta observed an inmate having problems at a table in chow hall, "A". "I saw my ADA worker, St. Michael, exiting chow hall "B" and called him over to assist the inmate. St. Michael went to the inmate in distress and then reported back to my colleague (another c/o) that we have a medic non-medical emergency. He needed to get to

the medical clinic. St. Michael ran with him from the chow hall to the clinic. Subsequently, the inmate had a stroke and was transferred to an outside hospital. Due to the assessment and action of St. Michael, it is quite possible that the inmate in crisis was saved."

8. 20 Nov. 2017: "Inmate came out of his cell, staggered, and fell down, hitting his head on the railing. This resulted in a large gash and severe bleeding on the left of his forehead. Inmate St. Michael, having witnessed the fall from the end of the tier, proceeded to the disabled inmate, using his t-shirt as a compress to stop the bleeding. He sat the inmate up and held the compression on until Medical Staff arrived. St. Michael explained, 'I kept the inmate in a seated position because of the serious cut and the bleeding, as well as the inmates

apparent disorientation.' The inmate was rushed to the hospital, where he stayed for four days."

9. In process of publishing the following:

a. Messenger's/Angels & Demons or Aliens

b. "C.N.E.W.; Christian Nations-Eagle Warriors

c. The History of Lucifer

d. Habeas Corpus Manual

CALIFORNIA PARALEGAL

Guidelines, Supporting Law, Hourly Wages

1. Lab C §515(a).

2. Cal C Reg Title. 8 §11040.

3. C.F.R. Sections §541.2007; §541.301(a)(d); §541.302.

4. For Expert Fees $483.00 an hour.

   a. Collins V. City of Los Angeles (2012) 205 Cal. App. 4th. 140

   b. Ellis V. Toshiba, American Information Systems Inc. (2013) 218 Cal. App. 4th 853.

   c. Guillory v. Hill (2019) 36 Cal. App. 5th. 208.

   d. Morris v. Hyundai Motor America (2019) 41 Cal. App. 5th 24.

5. California Paralegal Guide §2.06 B.

   a. Syers Properties III Ln V. Ramkin (2014) 266 Cal. App. 4th 691-702. Hourly rate, $150.00.

6. Recovery of cost in a criminal action.

a. PC §1054.9

b. Rubio v. Sup Ct. (2016) 244 Cal. App. 4th. 459.

7. Paralegal Licensing Requirements:

a. Paralegals must understand their function and maintain the highest standards of ethical conduct.

b. The legal assistant as well as anyone else working within the legal profession must be imbued with a high regard for the law and should seek to promote respect for the law so that it may be effective and survive.

c. Business and Professional code §6450.

8. Rules of Professional Conduct:

a. Ames v. State Bar, (1973) 8 Cal. 3rd 910. 917.

b. Miraoito v. Liccardo, (1992) 4 Cal. App. 4th 41, 44.

c. Stanely v. Richmond (1995) 35 Cal. App. 4th 1070, 1097.

d. Chambers v. Kay, (2002) 29 Cal. App. 4th 142, 161.

e. Fletcher v. Davis, (2004) 33 Cal. App. 4th 61, 71-72.

9. California State Bar:

   a. Business and Professional Code §6000; Rules of professional conduct.

   b. National Federation of Paralegal Association (N.F.P.A). Http://www.NFPA.org/code.ASPX

   c. National Association of Legal Assistants (N.A.L.A). Http://www.paralegals.org/associations/2270/files/model_code_of_ethics_09_06.pdf.

10. Education requirements of paralegals: Business and Professional Code §6450.

   a. What paralegals should not do:

      1. Give legal advice,

      2. Represent a client,

      3. Recommend the use of any legal documents,

      4. Not act as a runner,

      5. Not to engage in the practice of law,

      6. To set or establish fees to charge clients,

7. As a paralegal, you prepare all legal completed forms, motions, and briefs. This is given to the attorney with list of contents for the attorney to file in court for the client.

11. Paralegals must possess one of the following:

a. Certificate of completion of a paralegal program, approved by the American Bar Association.

   1. Obtain a degree from a postsecondary institution with a minimum of 24 credit hours or equivalent.

b. Bachelor's or advanced degree. Minimum of one years' experience.

c. Every two (2) years you are required to complete a four (4) hour course of continuing legal education in General Law or in an area in specialized law, plus four (4) hours of legal ethics. Business and Professional Code §6450(d).

12. Paralegal License:

C.N.E.W.—Dr. St. Michael

a. From county clerk: $175.00, plus $10.00 for ID.

b. To be renewed two (2) years.

C.N.E.W.—Dr. St. Michael

RESUME:

- Name: St. Michael D. Balzarini
- Date of Birth: 17 April 1972
- Place of Birth: Jackson County, Kansas City, Missouri.
- Both parents work for the Government:
  1. My father "Lewis", worked as an arrow space engineer for Rockdyne, in the Space race to the moon program.
  2. My mother "Lena", worked as a Lockheed Engineer at Skunkworks. She worked in the Cockpit for advanced U.S. Aircraft.
- Raised with 21 Arabian horses and my sister's welch pony.
- I had two (2) stallions', one named "Prince," and the other named "Fella."
- My German Shepherd was named Lebin.
- All of my horses and my dog along with over 2,000+ birds all responded to me when I called them.

- Third in regional for cross country running and won the State Fair for a Science Project.
- Trained in the following:
    a. U.S.A.F.: Cryptology and Communications (Purple-Heart).
    b. Telecom-Repair
    c. Lost wax casting and jewelry making.
    d. Took my weight class in boxing and weightlifting (Team Captain).
    e. Judicial Science: C.L.A. (Certified Legal Assistant associate degree).
    f. Vocational Building Maintenance.
    g. Vocational Graphic Arts.
    h. Vocational Internal Medicine; Ph.D. (Research degree).
    i. Master's degree in counseling
    j. T.A.B.A. Score: 12.9
    k. G.P.A (Grade Point Average): 97%-99%.

l. Teach apologetics and theological opinions.

m. Published one book and working on another.

n. Working on three (3) manuscripts to publish.

o. Member of MENSA

p. Organizer of a new group called "C.N.E.W." Christian Nations-Eagle Warriors.

q. Stamp collecting/philatelist

ARTICLES WRITTEN:

By: Dr. St. Michael

www.prisonsfoundation.org

1. (C.N.E.W) "Christian Nations-Eagle Warriors."
2. The Christian Faith
3. Three (3) Separate Creations
4. Teaching of the Seedline Theory.
5. What should we do until the Lord Returns?
6. How many crucified at crucifixion of Jesus Christ
7. Description of the events leading up to Jesus Christ's Death.

8. Knowledge: Commanded by God.

9. On the Bible.

10. On Evolution and for those who don't believe in 3 creations.

11. How to rescue America's Economic Condition.

12. Prayer service (Who we should pray to be heard by God).

13. The Seven Deadly Sins.

14. Evidence of Beliefs

15. The Question of Acts 17:26: "Made on Blood."

16. When was Jesus Christ Born: 29th September.

ESCHATOLOGY:

17. The Three (3) Visions of America (George Washington).

18. God's Judgement on America.

19. Family of God.

20. What's Apologetics?

21. In 2015: This Transpired to Me.

22. Inmate Programming and Assistance.

23. "People who attend religious services live longer," new study suggests.

24. In following Jesus (Yeshua).

25. The View's on Second Coming.

26. The 20 Religions compared to Biblical Christianity.

27. 2017: This Transpired.

28. Eschatological Prophecies of America Today (2016).

29. Gospel Beliefs in our last days.

30. Preparing Jesus Christs people for his soon return.

31. Divided Israel and God's Judgement on America on our beliefs.

32. Inmate programming and enhance program.

33. Jokes for humor.

34. Messengers/Angels + Demons

35. Nevi'im

C.N.E.W.—Dr. St. Michael

SUPPLEMENT: 2

Change in America is needed and what we can do…

    A. Congress declares Bible Word of God.

    B. Reading levels of Bibles

    C. Pet Bird

    D. We can do for changes.

C.N.E.W.—Dr. St. Michael

Pet Bird

What we were able to train Ellie to do

1. Come here.
2. Exercise: She would hold onto your hand and then she would flap her wings.
3. Fluff: She would do this on the blanket or paper and then fluff her feathers.
4. Water: She would go and get a drink.
5. Go home: This was to tell her to go to her cage.
6. Mummum: When asking her if she is hungry or wants something to eat.
7. Go Nana: This is when she would get up under my neck and go to sleep. If I went to sleep, she would do the same and just snuggle under my neck or on my shoulder.
8. Candy: This was not used often, but we would use this to entice her to do something. When you asked her, "you want candy?" she would go crazy for it.

9. Cookie: She liked cookies, only light-colored cookies, no chips, or dark cookies.

10. Cracker: If she was hungry, she would like crackers.

11. Get the paper: Place a paper down or a paper towel and tell her to get on it and fluff, or she would just play with the paper.

12. On my shoulder: I would tell her to get on my shoulder and she would sit and groom herself or beg for food. Sometimes she would even watch T.V.

13. Ellie: This was her name, and she would come when you called her unless she was tired. If she was tired, she would go to sleep on you or in her cage.

14. Get-up: I would put my hand in front of her feet and tell her to get up and she would get up on my hand.

15. To Me: She would to me to get food or to peck me.

16. Get-off: This is what I would say to tell her to get off my hand or my shoulder, and sometimes off the bed.

17. Bath: She liked warm water better then cold water. She would take a bath and put one leg in and back out, then in again and then both legs. She would put her head in and if the water was nice and warm, she would get soaked and then come back to me, trying to get dry and warm as she shivered.

18. Tell me a secret: If I said this, she would click her beak next to my ear or peck my ear and pretend like she was telling me something.

19. Get the lid: When she was hungry, we would place a tumbler lid on top of her food and then she would go and push, pick it up or push it out of the way to get her food so that she could eat.

This must be implemented immediately. The following applies to all Americans.

A. United States Constitution. Bill of Rights. Article I;XIV (1:14).

B. Congress declares Bible "The Word of God." The Bible is, "the rock on which our republic rests," Public Law 97-280. 4 October 1982.

C. We the people of the United States set forth the following to make all people safer.

1. All uniformed officers will not be allowed to carry lethal weapons. (Handguns are for killing people and you do not have that right.

2. Uniformed officers will wear body cameras and tasers or other non-lethal weapons.

3. Shotguns will remain in units for emergency and S.W.A.T as support units if needed, but only as a last resort.

4. All uniformed officers will work together to deescalate the situation and avoid violence.

5. Anyone who kills an officer will get the death penalty.

SUPPLEMENT: 3

A. Why curses on "America Starting-2016"and other info.

B. Vision again from Yehoshua.

C. Parables to learn and live by.

C.N.E.W.—Dr. St. Michael

2016

1. People need to cry out for repentance of sins. Jesus Christ will send His prophets before His coming in the great and dreadful day of our Lord Jesus Christ.

2. I am one of two with power to curse and heal. I have been sent to prepare His people for His return, (Rev. 1:7; Matt. 24:29-31).

3. Because you, America, refuse to turn the hearts of your fathers and children. You have not done the commandments of the Lord. All of you have turned away and spoken with unclean mouths against God.

4. I will strike America with terrible curses for her transgressions. You shall have no peace. O America, you are cursed and will find no mercy. All of you Godless shall be cursed. America is cursed until you repent. The elect will find forgiveness for their sins and will have His mercy. His people who abide in Him will receive salvation from their sins. You elect

will inherit the light of God until you fulfill your covenantal duties before your Lord Jesus Christ, (Eph. 2:10; Rom. 8:9-10). O America, it's the end of the world as you know it…You have become a reprobate nation from the top to the bottom. The Lord will continue to reign curses down upon you until America repents and turns its heart back to the Lord. Then I will pray to stop the curses, because the Lord loves all of you. I will pray and pray and pray for the repentance of America every day.

In my Master Jesus Christs service,

St. Michael

I am sent to teach about the Kingdom of God and to heal those who ask. I have been sent to prepare His people for His return.

Greetings my Friend.

I had a vision from God again and was told to share it with you…

God woke me up this morning around 2:30-3:00am. It is the 5th of November, and I am crying as I write this. What I saw made me cry and ask why it is that so many people in a few big cities were going to die. I heard people screaming and crying and burning really bad.

It made me cry out, "Why God?"

God said, "Let them know that they have time to repent and turn back to me."

For no reason, the shelf over my bed was dumped out onto my bed, which seems to have been another way for God to get my attention.

God said, "Tell them, for they have a short time."

America, you are cursed. Please turn back to God before it is too late…

In my Master Jesus Christs service,

St. Michael

What do they mean and how to apply it to your life today.

1. A lamp on a stand (Matt. 5:14-16; Mark 4:21-22; Luke 8:6-17;11:33-36).
2. The Wise and Foolish Builders (Matt. 7:24-27; Luke 6:47-49).
3. New Cloth as an Old Garment (Matt. 9:16; Luke 5:36).
4. New Wine in Old Wineskins (Matt. 9:17; Mark 2:22; Luke 5:37-38).
5. The Sower (Matt. 13:3-9; Mark 4:2-9; Luke 8:4-8).
6. The Weeds (Matt. 13:24-30; Mark 4:2-9; Luke 8:4-8).
7. The Mustard Seed (Matt. 13:31-32; Mark 4:30-32; Luke 13:18-19).
8. The Yeast (Matt. 13:33; Luke 13:20-21).
9. The Hidden Treasure (Matt. 13:44).
10. The Pearl (Matt. 13:45-46).
11. The Net (Matt. 13:47-50).

12. The Lost Sheep (Matt. 18:12-14; Luke 15:3-7).

13. The Unmerciful Servant (Matt. 18:23-35).

14. The Workers in the Vineyard (Matt. 20:1-16).

15. The Two Sons (Matt. 21:28-32).

16. The Tenants (Matt. 21:33-45; Mark 12:1-12; Luke 20:9-19).

17. The Wedding Banquet (Matt. 22:2-14).

18. The Ten Virgins (Matt. 25:1-13).

19. The Talents (Matt. 25:14-30).

20. The Growing Seed (Mark 4:26-29).

21. The Absent Householder (Mark 13:34-37).

22. The Creditor and the Two Debtors (Luke 7:41-43).

23. The Good Samaritan (Luke 10:30-37).

24. A Friend in Need (Luke 11:5-13).

25. The Rich Fool (Luke 12:16-21).

26. The Watchful Servants (Luke 12:35-40).

27. The Faithful Servant (Matt. 24:45-51; Luke 12:42-48).

28. The Barren Fig Tree (Luke 13:6-9).

29. The Place of Honor (Luke 14:7-11).

30. The Great Banquet (Luke 14:16-24).

31. The Cost of Being a Disciple (Luke 14:25-35).

32. The Lost Coin (Luke 15:8-10).

33. The Prodigal son (Luke 15:11-32).

34. The Shrewd Steward (Luke 16:1-13).

35. The Rich Man and Lazarus (Luke 16:19-31).

36. The Obedient Servant (Luke 17:7-10).

37. The Persistent Widow (Luke 18:1-8).

38. The Pharisee and the Tax Collector (Luke 18:9-14).

39. The Men Minas (Luke 19:11-27).

Matthew has 20 parables with 10 being unique to the book of Matthew.

Mark has 8 parables with 2 being unique to the book of Mark.

Luke has 27 parables with 17 being unique to the book of Luke.

SUPPLEMENT: 4

Historical and Theological Resources

A. Coat of Arms of Jesus Christs Genealogy

B. Jewish Encyclopedia; About Khazars

C. Pilate's report to Tiberius Caesar of the arrest, trial, and crucifixion of Jesus Christ.

Jews (Hebrew)

Theological and Historical Resources:

A. The thirteenth Tribe by Arthur Koestler.

B. Missing links discovered in Assyrian tablets by E. Raymond Capt.

C. 5 Vol. Lost Tribes to Israel Today by Steve M. Collins.

D. The Jews Khazaria by Kevin Alan.

Research material that answers skeptics.

Church of Israel
Rt. 1. Box 218E.
Schell City, MO 64783

Cliftona Emahiser's Teaching Ministry
1010 N. Vine St.
Fostoria, OH. 44830

God's Kingdom Ministries
6201 University Ave. N.E.
Fridley, MN. 55432

Church of Restoration of True Israel
Box 411373
Chicago, IL. 60641

Richard K. Hoskin Publishing Company
Box 997.

Lynchburg, VA. 24505

Sacred Truth Ministries
Box 18.
Mountain City, TN. 37683

Steven M. Collins
Box 88735.
Sioux Falls, SD. 57109-1005

Kingdom Ministries
Box 1021
Harrison, AR. 72602

Destin Publishing
Box 177.
Merrimack, MA. 01860-0177

1. The Apologetics Study Bible C.S.B. (2017) by Holman Bible Publishing. (Good present-day translation). Page 1363; What is the Christian Movement by R. Alan Streett (his opinion is biased and unsubstantiated. The scriptures cited in no way support his contention. It would be suggested that he or anyone else involved do further research and in-depth study on this subject.

2. Page 344 is, "Psychology Biblical." No it is not! There is nothing wrong with counseling and any other view would be liberal. Anything that alters ones state of consciousness by mixing potions (drugs) is forbidden. "Pharmakia," is witchcraft and sorcery. See www.godiscreator.com for more information.

3. "Reason and Revelation" is a monthly magazine that teaches apologetics. See www.apologeticspress.org if you are interested.

4. Reasonable Faith; https://www.reasonablefaith.org

5. Apologetics 315; https://apologetics315.com

6. Investigating Faith; https://www.LeeStrobel.com

7. Christian Research Journal; https://www.equip.org

8. American Scientific Affiliation;

    https://www.asa3.org/asa/index_left.html

9. The Poached Egg; https://www.thepoachedegg.net

10. Gath (Bible) Archaeological Project;

    garth.wordpress.com

SUPPLEMENT: 5

1. Body Temple of God
2. On the subject of human relationships
3. For your health and soul; Bible and Health
4. Divine Diet
5. Junk Food made me do it
6. Worlds Healthiest Diet
7. Are Vegetarians Healthier? Yes
8. Protein
9. Eating for optimum health
10. Nutrition through macrobiotics
11. Swine as food
12. Cancer cure
13. Common abbreviations for blood tests
14. Misc herbs for health

Body Temple of God

1. 1 Cor. 3:16-17: "Know ye not that ye are the temple of God and that the Spirit of God dwelleth in you. If any man defiles the temple of God, him shall God destroy; for the temple of God is Holy, which temple ye are, (1 Cor. 3:16-17; John 3:1-3). This means believers are the temple of God for the indwelling of the Holy Spirit. To corrupt the temple of God comes with a solemn warning against sexual sin, alcoholic drinks, tobacco, and narcotics. All of these destroy the body.

2. Being Lacto-Oval-Vegetarian means eating no red meat, chicken, or pork. Why do we desecrate our bodies by eating unnatural and unclean food stuffs? This is unpleasing to our bodies as well as to Jesus Christ. If we truly love Jesus Christ, we will take care of this temple-body that He gave us to take care of. I implore you to try it for 30 days or longer. I had

a doctor come to my room in the year 2020. The Doctor asked others and me how we were doing. After testing positive for Covid-19 and being resolved, the doctor looked at the paper about me and said, "You're one of those." I said, "What do you mean?" He said, "You look younger than your age." I said, "I'll take that." I was in the room with just a t-shirt and shorts on. Taking of my shirt, I asked, "How's this?" The doctor said, "I've been all over this prison and I have not seen anyone who looks like you." He said, "How did you get in shape like a body builder in here?" I told him that between the workouts, no fat and a six pack as well as being on a diet and prayer. I gave all glory to my Lord Jesus Christ.

3. A lady came from the government and asked the corrections officer to back away. She stated that this was private. She asked about my family and where I

was born. She showed me a picture of a relative who I looked like from the 1870's with long hair on his face. I asked for a copy, and she told me to get it from a website called Ancestry. She asked me what year I was born and said, "1848, 1928, 1952, 1972, all on April 17th. I believe it's 1972." My reply was, "You need to read Matthew 16:28." After I said this, she said, have a nice day and left.

On the subject of Human Relationships

1. In humans, 98% of people do not know the difference between sex and making love.

    a. Sex: The woman lays down and the guy gets on top and after a few minutes, gets off. (Eros). This is animal sex plain and simple. Most of the time the woman is not satisfied.

    b. Making love: You place the woman face down. You massage her body from her neck to the toes. You kiss and lick everything in the process of doing this.

2. Then, roll her over onto her back and repeat the process. There are six triggers that make a woman scream in ecstasy. As research and science have shown, when the woman wakes up the next day, her whole body will scream with joy and ecstasy. If her vagina could talk, it would say, "I feel so alive," and

it would scream with joy, "Oh yes! I am alive! I am alive!" This level of maturity is agape.

For your Health and Soul

Vegetarian diet by eating a big breakfast as well as a big lunch, dinner, and salad. Later, when you are hungry, drink or eat fruits and vegetable juices. Watch your health change. This is because your diet affects your life, (John 2:21; Rom. 12:1; 1 Cor. 6:19; 1 Thess. 5:23).

Exercise and Supplements

Take 1,000 milligrams of Vitamin C four times a day as well as 500 milligrams of B-12 and smilax two times a day.

A. The relationship between dietetic habits and physical and moral condition. Ignatius Press. Box 1339, Ft. Collins, CO. 80522.

B. Market Food for Life (64) by Max Tores

C. Free to be Thin (79) by Maria Chapian and Neva Coyles

D. 3D Diet by Carol Showalter

E. The Makers Diet (or Bible Diet) by Jordan Rubin

F. What would Jesus Eat by Don Colberts

G. The More-With-Less cookbook by Mary B. Lind

H. The Devil Wants me Fat by C.S. Lovetts

I. Pray your weight away by Charlie Shedd.

As a Christian, avoid unclean food, tobacco, and alcohol. Exercise and your average life span will be 20 years longer than others.

SUPER BLAST RECIPE

- Mix Vitamin C and B-12 into powder.
- Put 4-6 drops of smilax extract
- Place in the Microwave until dry.
- Eat about 15 minutes before a workout.

www.heraldpress.com (1-800-245-7895).

CANCER CURE?

Dear friends, I received this quite some time ago and thought I might put it in our newsletter. I watched a video of an Italian doctor who proved that cancer is a fungus and that he had been successfully treating cancer patients with "baking soda." Anyway, below is what some people believe is part of his "cancer cure formula." I want our readers to research this matter out and provide me with any helpful data you may find. Some people I know now believe that this formula just may be a very positive aid in the fight against cancer. Some of you people are good researchers. Anyway, below is the "baking soda and maple syrup" possible remedy for cancer.

The Maple Syrup and Baking Soda Remedy (how it works)

This formula is a combination of pure, 100% grade A maple syrup, baking soda and head. When mixed together and head for 10 minutes, causing the maple syrup and baking soda to bind together, the sugar content of the maple syrup is drawn to the damaged cells (which consume 15 times more glucose than normal cells), and the baking soda, which pulled into the cell along with the maple syrup kill the fungus inside the cell, which is highly acidic. The maple syrup and baking soda are very alkaline and force a rapid shift in the pH of the cell.

The Protocol

Very Important Note: Do not use baking soda which has aluminum added to it, or other harmful chemicals. Purchase a product which specifically states it does not contain aluminum or other chemicals. You will most likely need to purchase this product at a health food store, or online (Look for Bob's Red Mill, Aluminum-Free Baking Soda).

Instructions

Mix on part baking soda with three parts (pure 100% grade A) maple syrup in a small double boiler saucepan. (Note, you can mix it by the tablespoon, or by the cup depending on how many will be using it right away. Warning: Be sure the ratio is three to one). Note: Using it freshly made is best as keeping it overnight tends to allow it to eventually separate (the syrup and the soda).

While heating, stir briskly, keeping the temperature as close to 120 degrees as possible. Warning: Make sure not to overheat. (Note: As you are stirring, you will notice that the mixture will begin to foam. It takes at least 10 minutes for the foam to dissipate and turn into a brown looking syrup). It is now ready to use. **Use 1 teaspoon daily, or twice daily if the condition is severe.**

The bicarbonate maple syrup treatment: Dr. Tulio Simoncini acknowledges that cancer cells gobble up sugar, so when you encourage the intake of sugar, it is like sending in a trojan horse. The sugar is not going to end up encouraging the further growth of the cancer colonies because the baking soda is going to kill the cells before they have a chance to grow. The bicarbonate present is received by the cancer cells, which at first, are going to love the present. But not for long! This treatment is a combination of pure, 100% grade A maple syrup and aluminum free baking soda and was first reported on the Cancer Tutor site. (Take 1 teaspoon daily is what is suggested by the Cancer Tutor, but one could probably do this several times a day).

"There is not a tumor on God's green earth that cannot be licked with a little baking soda and maple syrup." This is the astonishing claim of controversial folk healer, Jim Kelmun, who says that this simple home remedy can stop and reverse the deadly growth of cancers. His loyal patients swear by the man they fondly call, Dr. Jim and say he is a miracle worker. "Dr. Jim cured me of lung cancer," said farmer Ian Roadhouse. "Those other doctors told me that I was a goner and had less than six months to live. But the doc put me on his mixture and in a couple of months, the cancer was gone. It did not even show up on the x-rays."

Dr. Jim discovered this treatment accidentally when he was treating a family plagued by breast cancer. There were five sisters in the family and four of them had died of breast cancer. He asked the remaining sister if there was anything different in her diet and she told him that she was partial to sipping maple syrup and baking soda. Since then, reported by a newspaper in Ashville, North Carolina, Dr. Jim dispensed this remedy to over 200 people diagnosed with terminal cancer and amazingly, he claims that 185 of those 200 people lived at least 15 more years and nearly half enjoyed a complete remission of their disease.

It is very important not to use baking soda which has had aluminum added to it. One can buy a product which specifically states it does not include aluminum or other chemicals. (e.g., Bob's Red Mill, Aluminum-Free, Baking Soda). Sodium bicarbonate is safe, extremely inexpensive, and unstoppably effective when it comes to cancer tissues. It is an irresistible chemical, acting as a sort of cyanide to cancer cells. It hits the cancer cells with a shock wave of alkalinity which allows much more oxygen into the cancer cells than they can tolerate. Cancer cells cannot survive in the presence of high levels of oxygen.

"The therapeutic treatment of bicarbonate salts can be administered orally, through aerosol, intravenously and through a catheter for direct targeting of tumors," says oncologist Dr. Tullio Simoncini. "Sodium bicarbonate administered orally, via aerosol or intravenously can achieve positive results only in some tumors, while others—such as the serious ones of the brain or the bones remain unaffected by the treatment."

The maple syrup enables and increases penetration of bicarbonate into all compartments of the body, even those which are difficult or impossible to penetrate by other means. These compartments include the central nervous system (CNS), through the blood-brain barrier, joints, solid tumors, and perhaps even the eyes. The maple syrup will make tissues more permeable. It will transport the bicarbonate across the blood-brain barrier and every other barrier in the body for sugar is universally needed by all cells in the body. Bicarbonate maple syrup treatments use the rabid growth mechanisms of the cancer cell against them.

Dr. Jim did not have contact with Dr. Simoncini and did not know that he is the only oncologist in the world who would sustain the combining of sugar with bicarbonate. Dr. Simoncini always directs his patients to dramatically increase sugar intake with his treatments but has never thought to mix the two directly by cooking them together because his treatments depend on interventionist radiologists who insert catheters to direct the bicarbonate as close to the affected area as possible, or physicians willing to do expensive intravenous treatments. When using these substances, it is safer to change one's vocabulary and not say one is treating and curing cancer. It is far better to conceptualize that one is treating and curing cancer. Far better to conceptualize that one is treating the infectious aspect of cancer, the fungus and yeast colonies and the yeast like bacteria that are the cause of TB.

Dr. Simoncini says that "In some cases, the aggressive power of fungi is so great as to allow it, with only a cellular ring made up of three units, to tighten to its grip, capture and kill its prey in a short time, notwithstanding the prey's desperate struggling. Fungus, which is the most powerful and the most organized micro-organism known, seems to be an extremely logical candidate as a cause of neoplastic proliferation."

PH of the blood is the most important factor to determine the state of the microorganisms in the blood. "Sodium bicarbonate therapy is harmless, fast, and effective because it is extremely diffusible. A therapy with bicarbonate for cancer should be set up with a strong dosage, continuously, and with pause less cycles in a destruction work which should proceed from the beginning to the end without interruption for at least 7-8 days. In general, a mass of 2-3-4 centimeters will begin to consistently regress from the third to the fourth day, and collapses from the fourth to the fifth," says Dr. Simoncini.

"There are many ways to use sodium bicarbonate and it is a universal drug like iodine and magnesium chloride. Raising pH increases the immune system's ability kill bacteria," concludes a study conducted at The Royal Free Hospital and School of Medicine in London. Viruses and bacteria that cause bronchitis and colds thrive in an acidic environment. To fight a respiratory infection and dampen symptoms such as a runny nose and sore throat, taking an alkalizing mixture of sodium bicarbonate and potassium bicarbonate will certainly help.

The apple cider vinegar ¼ teaspoon and ¼ teaspoon of baking soda taken 2 times or more a day is another treatment, as is lemon and baking soda, or lime and baking soda formulas. Perhaps honey could be substituted for maple syrup for those who live in parts of the world where maple syrup is not available but to my knowledge, no on has experimented with this.

The breakdown of glucose or glycogen produces lactate and hydrogen ions—for each lactate molecule, one hydrogen ion is formed. The presence of hydrogen ions, not lactate, makes the muscle acidic and it will eventually cause a halt of muscle function. As hydrogen ion concentrations increase, the blood and muscle become acidic. This acidic environment will slow down enzyme activity and ultimately, the breakdown of glucose itself. Acidic muscles will aggravate associated nerve endings causing pain and increase irritation of the central nervous system. The athlete may become disoriented and feal nauseous. By buffering acidity in the blood, bicarbonate draws more of the acid produced within the muscle cells out into the blood and thus reduce the level of acidity within the muscle cells themselves.

By: Mark Sircus Ac., OMD

Director International Medical Veritas Association. This article is from the 850-page e-book, "Winning the War on Cancer." This article has been purposely edited so as to make it user friendly to the common man and woman who are looking for answers.

C.N.E.W.—Dr. St. Michael

APPENDIX: Some Common Abbreviations:

https://www.nlm.nih.gov/medlineplus/appendixb.html

Medline Plus:

Blood-Tests:

WBC—White Blood Cell

RBC—Red Blood Cell

MCV—Mean Corpuscular Volume

MCH—Mean Corpuscular Hemoglobin

MCHC—Mean Corpuscular Hemoglobin Concentration

HGB—Hemoglobin

AST—Aspartate Aminotransferase

ALT—Alanine Aminotransferase

HCV—Hepatitis C Virus

TSH—Thyroid Stimulating Hormone

LDL—Low Density Lipoprotein

HDL—High Density Lipoprotein

PSA—Prostate Specific Antigen

HIV—Human Immunodeficiency Virus

HPV—Human Papilloma Virus

CHD—Congenital Heart Disease

CBC—Complete Blood Count

LFT—Liver Function Test (Bilirubin; Phosphatase {Alkaline}; Albumin; Alanine & Aspartate, Prothrombin).

TRUP—Transurethral Resection of Prostate Gland

PLT—Platelet Count

PT—Prothrombin Time

ANA—Antibodies

Cr—Kidney

Miscellaneous Herbs for Health

FLUX:

How to reduce chlorofluorocarbon (CFCS), which harms ozone layer. Clean electronic circuit boards with "Lemon Juice", as a flux, it is a safer flux, no more heavy resin flex, or being cited for improper storage.

WART REMOVAL: Mixture of Podophyllum and Benzoin. Podophyllum, known as mandrake, devils apple, hog apple, umbrella plant, wild lemon, tincture of benzoin is alcoholic solution. Mix a teaspoon of podophyllum which has been ground to powder form in about a quarter ounce of tincture of benzoin mix thoroughly until power dissolved, apply to warts, and watch them disappear in a few days.

WITCH HAZEL: The bush Hamamelis, leaves are distilled with diluted alcohol to produce what is called Hamamelis water or witch hazel. Witch hazel has been found to help with a number of problems, from Acne to sunburns as well as a makeup remover and clearing up hemorrhoids.

ALOE: With some 170 different species, the dried juice of the leaves was first used as an ingredient in drug mixtures to induce bowel movements. Secondly, as a healing ointment applied to burns and cuts.

PURPLE FOXGLOVE: Known as digitalis purpurea from the dried flowers came a heart medication by the name of Digoxin to treat cardiac irregularities.

SLIPPERY ELM: Or known Ulmus fulva. A warm infusion of the bark was discovered to relieve throat irritations.

JIMSON: (AKA Jamestown Weed): Datura Stramonium: From its dried leaves and flowering tops come the drug Stramonium which is used as a bronchial dilator for relief of Asthma.

MEADOWSWEET: Rheumatism, Arthritis, and fever.

GOLDENSEAL: Stops bleeding and even hemorrhaging. It was used by the Cherokee Indians. It is also known as Eye root, ground raspberry, Indian dye, yellow puccoon, and yellow Indian paint. By pulverizing the rhizome (underground stem), of the plant or powder, place on cut, or mix with water and drink for hemorrhaging.

SORE THROAT CURE (aka Privet): Boil cup of ground privet leaves in a pan of water and then filter through a cloth. When this is done and the extract has cooled down, use as a throat gargle.

Cleaning Copper: The cheap and easy way is to use vinegar on a cloth or a rag and then dip this in salt. Rub this on your tarnished copper. Salt and vinegar scrubs away the tarnish and leaves the copper like new.

HORSERADISH (Amoracia Lapathifolia): Horseradish and a proportionate amount of hydrogen peroxide and add to polluted water. In a half an hour, the pollutants will be neutralized. Forming insoluble polymers which can easily be filtered from the water.

($920 to treat 66,000 gallons of Phenol contaminated water. Dr. Jean-Marc Bollang, Penn State Agricultural Sciences, Research Associate, Jersey-Dec, Penn States Center for Bioremediation, and detoxification.

JUNE: FULL MOON: Strawberry moon, flower moon, rose moon and honeymoon. The term honeymoon originally referred to the full moon of the wedding or the rest of the lunar month (waning moon) after it, which occurs nearest to the summer solstice and the first day of summer. If there is a haze present, as there usually is on June nights, the low moon will be dimmed and turned to a rich golden honey colored moon.

WILLOW TREE: Salicylic acid is what is used to make what we know as aspirin today however willow bark is known to have been used as far back to the time of Hippocrates in 400 B.C. People during this time would take the bark of a willow tree and would chew on it in order to reduce a fever or to reduce any inflammation that they may have been dealing with. Willow bark has been used all over the world, including in China as well as all over Europe.

SALICYLIC ACID: Or Acetylsalicylic acid (ASA) or just plain aspirin.

HIGH MALLOW (MALVA SYLVESTRIS): Soothing for indigestion, heartburn, and stomach problem.

TEA: Made with 1 tablespoon of leaves, stem, root, and flower which is put into a cup of cool water and left to sit for a few hours.

PURPLE CONE (Echinacea Purpurea and Echinacea Angustifolia): Give yourself a rinse in Echinacea justice before the exhibition of walking on fire or plunging your hand in boiling water.

-Cures: Headaches, toothaches, insect, and snake bites. Colds and flu and pain in joints.

-A Tea: 5-ounces of dried herb and then 15.5 ounces of grain alcohol. Ever clear is okay. 7.5 ounces of distilled water, mix and let set for 2 weeks.

C.N.E.W.—Dr. St. Michael

SUPPLEMENT: 6

Christian topics for your growth and study.

Review everything you read…

A. Three (3) separate creations.

B. Superfetation

C. Seven deadly sins and Saligia

D. Christianity and Psychiatry

E. Jokes to make you laugh or not?

Three (3) Separate Creations:

By: St. Michael

The first and original creation is from the dateless past to the end, because Angels ruled various planets as seen in Isaiah 14:12-14; Ezekiel 28:11-17, Col. 1:15-18, 2 Peter 3:5-6. We see the original first creation, as per Dt. 32:4, Job 38, Ps. 18:30, Ecc. 3:11 and was made perfect and inhabited (Isaiah 45:18).

The world, cosmos and social system that came forth is then that which embraces the whole pre-Adam universe, to which all fossils and these remains belong (2 Peter 3:5-8, Jeremiah 4:23-26). The Earth was made chaos, this ended Earth's first perfect state and began it's first sinful chosen pursuit. This earth (Hebrew, "Hayah") became (Hebrew, "Tohu Va Bohu") wasted and empty after Lucifer's rebellion against God. They were created in the beginning before the earth was (Genesis 1:1, Job 38:4-7) but during the chaos caused by Lucifer's rebellion, they were forbidden to give light on earth until judgement had been completed (Isa. 14:12-14; Jeremiah 4:23-26, Ezekial 28:11-17, 2 Peter 3:5-8). In Genesis 1, the beasts were brought into being or created and then men and women were created after, thereby, making all races.

The (2) Separate Creations

In Genesis 1:27, the Second Creation, we see that God created all men in His image. (In Hebrew "bara" means to create, and "tselem" means shade resemblance). God created all men and women in His image at this time.

In Genesis 2:7, we see the third creation of man. So there is no confusion on God's creation of all races, in Genesis 1:27 and man being formed in Genesis 2:7 we see the Hebrew word meaning to mold or squeeze into shape as a potter does as the word "yatsar," (2 Kings 19:17, Psalm 94:9, 95:5, Isaiah 45:18). The Hebrew word for mud, rubbing or earth and dust is "aphar and the word for lives and breath of lives is "Chayim," because it made the body, the soul, and the spirit live and function together.

Adam in Hebrew means ruddy, to flush or turn rosy or red and so we see this denotes Adam's origin as being formed or made from the dust of Adamah, ground or red soil. so in Genesis 2:7, we have Adam being formed and then Genesis 2:15, the garden is made before man was placed in it and everything was completed.

Then, in Genesis 2:21-22, we see the woman being made out of already existing material—man, because Eve was taken out of the man, Adam (the Hebrew word for built or skillfully formed is "panah" and the Hebrew term "Ish shah" means of man or man with the womb or female), (1 Corinthians 11:3-12, 1 Timothy 2:9-15).

So we see the differences in the Creations which become apparent by God's word. In Genesis 1:27 and Genesis 2:7, we continue, but with only two words, "beast" and "formed". The beasts of the earth are used in Genesis 1 and the beast of the field in Genesis 2. We see in the third creation, after Adam is formed, that the field is the result of the labor of man or, as is the case of Eden, by God and this implication is that this beast in the third creation had a specific function which was to tend the cultivated fields. These two distinctly separate creations derive from the separate words that are used to describe their creation.

In the second creation, in the image of Elohim and in the third creation, which was the forming of Adam by Yahweh God. This marks clearly the separate processes that were applied to Adam and the process applied by Elohim in the second creation. This forming of man by God is confirmed in the comments in Jeremiah 1:4 and are stated by God.

In other variations, there emerges between these creations the fact that the third creation saw the breath of God blown into the nostrils of Adam and not into the second creation. We see that the female of Genesis 1:27 was created when man was created and, making this a simultaneous event, they were told to procreate and to replenish the earth. This was an order that would extend to all of humanity for all time.

Even was the first woman made from Adam's flesh (or D.N.A) and this occurred a long time after Adam had been formed by God. This came about after Adam had already been assigned a task to perform and then was instructed by God, as can be seen in Genesis 2:16-18. These instructions that were given to Adam by God were given for the purpose of preparing for the third separate creation. We see in the second creation was not instructed or levied with any laws, nor offered any firm admonitions about their behavior, other than to replenish and have dominion over every living thing.

All of the races of men and women were given free rein and simply told to live off of the land, eating nuts and fruit. At this time, there was not mandatory task or stipulations set out for living, or what could or could not live. In the third creation, a considerable lapse of time had occurred following the creation of man and women. It seems that God was not satisfied with that which he had done, and then decided to modify somethings upon the earth. This time, he recognized that there was no man to till the ground and rather than granting all that was already created inhibited rein, God set geographic boundaries and then established a basis for Adan's survival in Eden.

As to Eden's location it would be wise to read Dt. 29:29, and most likely destroyed in the Flood. In these two different creations, we see God had instructed Adam to follow the Laws, which was setting up the rules of Adam's obedience to God, and we also see the weakness of the human flesh, for Eve was made of flesh while Adam was made of the Earth.

It was Eve that induced and introduced death to the world, and to all of God's creations.

THE SEVEN DEADLY SINS

According to our Bible, sin entered the world in Adam's fall and all of mankind became innately sinful. For this and for actual sins committed, man becomes guilty and in need of salvation. Since sin is rooted in character and will, each sinner bears personal responsibility, hence the need for repentance. The views as to what constitutes sin vary, being partly determined by Church authority, social standards, and one's own conscience. But, in reality, sin is defined from our Bible!

The traditional "seven deadly sins" are pride, covetousness, lust, envy, gluttony, anger, and sloth. The Roman Catholic Church defines a mortal sin as a serious sin committed willingly and with clear knowledge of the wrongness.

We now turn to Proverbs. "These six things doth the Lord hate. Yehovah, hates six things, but there is a seventh things that he hates the worst of all," (Proverbs 6:16). This numerical form of proverb, to which the name of Middah is given by the letter writes is, goes as follows: A proud look he has ever detested, for such a look renders a man unfit for the reception of grace. A lying tongue betrays a deceitful heart. This heart of deceit soon joins hands with those who plot the shedding of innocent blood. The shedding of blood emboldens a man's heart to every evil imagination and the pursuit of every evil mischief.

The pursuit of such a man has grave implications for the covenant community, for this man's lies produce continuous discord among brethren. The forward man, (which in Hebrew is "luwz" meaning perverse or one who turns aside). It was also used as a cross with sweeping arches and the angles of gothic design, marked at the top by the word, "saligin," which was the pneumonic device for remember the seven deadly sins in medieval Europe. It also spelled, with the first letter in the Latin spelling for each sin. Beneath this, at the center of the cross, was a wide circle which was engraved with the "eye of God" which is refracted and distorted through a prism. Beneath this stirring image is another plague, which reads the words "Caue dus videt," which means "beware God sees."

JOKES TO MAKE YOU LAUGH OR NOT?

1. ON THE QUESTION OF WHICH WAS FIRST, THE CHICKEN OR THE EGG.

   a. A Chicken and Egg check into a cheap motel room. Moments later, the chicken sits up against the headboard and lights a cigarette. The egg says, "Well, that settles that."

2. HOW DO YOU TELL WHO IS A CITY BOY OR A COUNTRY BOY

   a. How do you tell the age of Horses?

   b. By the teeth.

   c. How do you tell the age of a tree?

   d. You drill a hole for a sample and count the rings.

   e. Isn't that the same way you tell the age of a person? Unless the rings have been rubbed out…

3. A woman's business has gone bust, and she is in dire financial straits. She decides to ask God for help. "God, please let me win the lottery." Lottery

night comes and somebody else wins. She prays again the next night. "God, please let me win the lottery!" The lottery comes, and she still has no luck. One last time she prays. "My God, why have you forsaken me? Please let me win the lottery so I can get my life back in order." Suddenly, there is a blinding flash of light and the voice of God fills the room and says, "Sweetheart, work with me on this—buy a ticket."

4. HOW I LEARNED THE BUSINESS—By: Cadet

A group of correctional cadets were walking past a prison facility the other day and all of the inmates began shouting, "19! 19! 19!" The fence was too high to see over, but one of the cadets saw a little gap in the fence, so he looked through to see what was going on. When he looked back at the other cadets, he was covering his eye with his hand and said, "Some idiot poked me in the eye with a stick!"

After he said this, the other inmates started shouting, "20! 20! 20!"

5. HOW I DID ON MY PSYCH TEST AS A CADET

During my visit to the mental asylum for my psych evaluation, I asked the psych doctor "how do you determine whether or not an inmate should be institutionalized".

"Well," said the psych doctor, "we fill up a bathtub and then we offer a teaspoon, a teacup, and a bucket to the inmate and tell them to empty the tub."

"Oh, I understand," said the cadet, "a normal inmate would use the bucket because it's bigger than the spoon or the teacup."

"No," said the psych doctor, "a normal inmate would pull the plug. Would you like a bed by the window?"

C.N.E.W.—Dr. St. Michael

"No, because the psych test doesn't apply to the c/o's."

SUPPLEMENT: 7

San Quentin, Prison, and Covid-19 as well as deaths throughout the C.D.C.R, prison fine with ignoring protocols.

1. S.Q turned down free covid test.

2. Listing of California prisons and P.I.A's

3. Coronavirus: Outbreak

4. C.D.C.R approved vendors.

5. C.C.O.P.A-Union attempts to recall Governor Newsom

C.N.E.W.—Dr. St. Michael

www.ingramcontent.com/pod-product-compliance
Lightning Source LLC
Chambersburg PA
CBHW052143070526
44585CB00017B/1946